THE STORY OF FRANK AND ANN SUTHERLAND

BY
ROBERT SUTHERLAND &
JOHN SUTHERLAND

NPH

Nazarene Publishing House
Kansas City, Missouri

BEHIND THE SILENCE

1999—2000 NWMS READING BOOKS

RESOURCE BOOK FOR THE LEADER
IMAGINE THE FUTURE
Edited by Beverlee Borbe

FOR THE READER

BEHIND THE SILENCE
The Story of Frank and Ann Sutherland
By Robert Sutherland and John Sutherland

BUILDING ON GOD'S FOUNDATION
50 Years of Alabaster
Edited by Tim Crutcher

JUST AROUND THE CORNER
Compassion in San Bernardino
By Robin Hyde as told to Cynthia Sherer

LOYD AND NITA MARTZ
Pioneers in Volunteer Missions
By Lela Morgan

PORTUGAL: A PLACE OF REFUGE
By Maria João Guerreiro

THROUGH HIS EYES
The Story of Youth in Mission
Edited by Ken Couchman and Jason E. Vickers

CONTENTS

Robert Sutherland, the third son of Frank and Ann Sutherland, was born during their first term as missionaries in China. In 1936 he returned to China with them on their second term. The family returned to the United States in 1941, six months before the bombing of Pearl Harbor. He is an active member of Sacramento First Church of the Nazarene, Sacramento, California.

John Sutherland, the oldest child of Frank and Ann, was also born in China during his parents' first term. He and his wife, Lucille, spent two terms in Africa as medical missionaries. They now live in Tucson, Arizona, and attend the Oro Valley Church of the Nazarene.

PROLOGUE

The banner gracing a small storefront Nazarene church in downtown Victoria, British Columbia, announced revival services with Evangelist J. T. Little. Looking back, no one could have anticipated what God was doing through those services. Then again, that's one of the reasons we have revivals—to provide a special setting in which the Spirit can accomplish what we otherwise thought to be impossible.

Two Canadian soldiers listened to Rev. Little declare that complete consecration to God brought spiritual freedom. He called it "entire sanctification." One soldier, a former minister in another denomination, had never heard anything like this before. He responded to an invitation and consecrated his life to God. His name was Francis Campbell Sutherland.

Neither Francis (later called Frank) nor his future wife, Ann Findlay Bowman—who would also respond at a later time to the invitation—could have anticipated the results of this commitment. For the moment, however, World War I was in its third year, and in just a few weeks Frank would leave Canada for the trenches of northern France.

✳   ✳   ✳

This is a true story about Frank and Ann Sutherland—a story of two lives brought together from opposite ends of Canada by the so-called fortunes of war. Drawn together by love and united in marriage, Frank and Ann lived out their commitment to God without reservation.

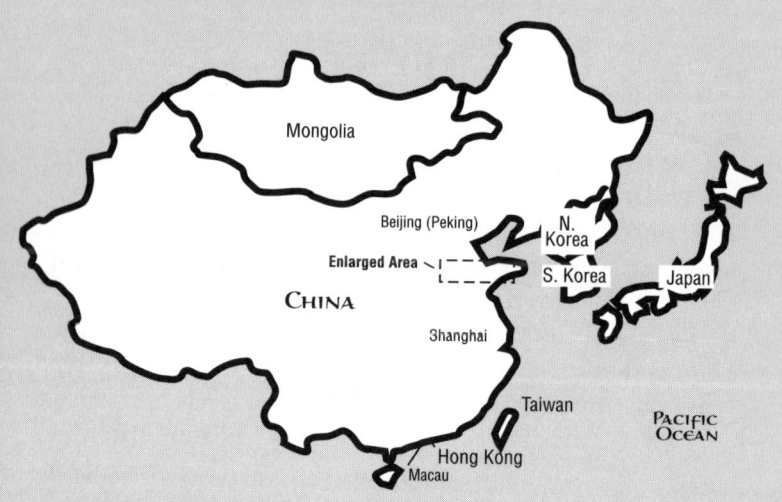

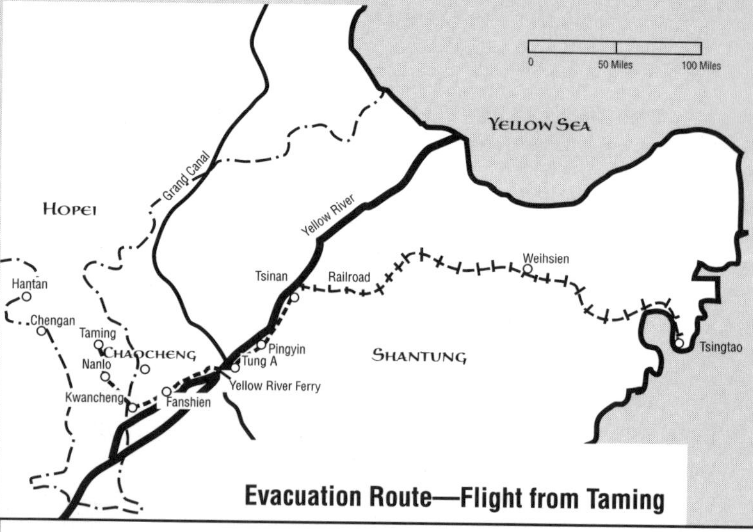

Evacuation Route—Flight from Taming

1st night	Nanlo	8th-9th nights	Tung A
2nd night	Kwancheng	10th-11th nights	Pingyin
3rd-5th nights	Fanshien	12th night	On board train
6th night	Slept on board boat	13th	Arrived Tsingtao
7th night	Chinese Inn		

Chapter 1

CANADIAN ROOTS

Frank Sutherland

Francis Campbell Sutherland was born in Richmond, Quebec, in 1887. With his parents and two younger and adoring sisters, Frank attended St. Anne's Anglican Church in Richmond. Frank, as our mother always called him, also worked in his father's drugstore and, as a young man, developed a love for cameras and photographic equipment. Little did he know his fascination with photography would one day be put to good use on the mission field.

In the fall of 1906, Frank entered McGill University in Montreal. He graduated four years later with a bachelor of arts degree. Following college, he taught for two years, first as principal of Danville Academy and then as principal of Ormstown Academy. Both academies are in Quebec's Eastern Townships, a part of the province south of the St. Lawrence River.

In 1911 Sir Lomer Gouin, premier of the Province of Quebec, appointed Frank's father as inspector general of Protestant education for the province, and later that year, the family moved to Quebec City. Then, in the fall of 1912, Frank resumed his studies both at McGill and at McGill's Montreal Diocesan Theological College. In 1915 he earned a master of arts from McGill and a licentiate in sacred theology from the Diocesan College.

The Anglican Church ordained Frank in 1915, after which he became parish priest at Spirit River, Alberta, under the bishop of Athabasca. Spirit River, then a frontier settlement of log houses and dirt streets, lies 30 miles east of Dawson Creek and the start of the Alaska Highway (for a short time known as the Alcan Highway). Frank ministered mostly to rough and hardy frontiersmen.

But rather than his being intimidated, the raw land and sturdy people of Spirit River enlivened the young Easterner. In the face of difficult times, Frank tried earnestly to minister to their needs. Sadly, very few of them attended services.

Frank felt the formal liturgies of the church failed to address the realities of frontier life. Hoping to make the love of Jesus real to these men, Frank adopted a more informal type of service. But when word of Frank's approach reached church authorities, the bishop rushed to Spirit River to confront the young priest and bring him back to the ancient liturgies. Frank stoutly maintained his position, even to the point of offering his resignation. Surprisingly, the bishop accepted on the spot, leaving Frank uncertain about his future.

Frank resigned in 1916, while World War I still raged in Europe. Canada continued to send her share of men to the trenches of France. A pacifist at heart but anxious to serve, Frank opted to become a stretcher bearer. He enlisted and began training at Central Mobilization Camp Sidney on Vancouver Island, British Columbia.

Ann Findlay Bowman

In 1901 Archibald Murdock Bowman relocated his family from Glasgow, seeking a better life in Canada. The Bowmans, having found Alberta's winters harsh and the soil poor, soon moved to Sidney, British Columbia. Far from Alberta's bleak prairie land, the family now enjoyed an ideal setting of meadows, forests, mountains, and sea, with a climate warmed by the Japanese Current.

Ann's father found work on Ardmore Estates, a few miles north of Sidney. He became manager of the estates a few years later. Here, the children had use of a dock and rowboats, and they also had access to the beach. The Bowmans attended the Presbyterian Church in Sidney, traveling to Sunday worship in a horse-drawn buggy.

Frank and Ann

Frank, along with other soldier friends, visited Sidney's Presbyterian Church. Ann's mother often invited these soldiers, Frank among them, for Sunday dinner. Ann and another teenage sister, Maggie, introduced their soldier guests to the rowboats, the beach, and swimming. Unfortunately, Frank could not swim well, as Quebec's swift-flowing St. Francis River had not invited swimming.

However, Frank could hike. Mount Newton rose 1,000 to 1,500 feet near Ardmore Estates, and along its fern-bordered trails the friendship between Ann and Frank blossomed. But after the completion of training at Sidney, Frank's unit transferred to Victoria for embarkation to Europe. The move separated the new friends.

The Church of the Nazarene

Along with his close friend, David Phillips, Frank looked for a place to worship in Victoria. David was Pentecostal, but they could not find any Pentecostal churches in Victoria. Instead, they attended the Church of the Nazarene. Here, Frank heard and responded to Rev. Little's message of full salvation.

In the meantime, rumors indicated they would soon sail for England. The army granted leave, and Frank traveled across Canada to visit his family in Quebec. Returning to Sidney in January 1917, he again marveled at the vast roll and sweep of land in the prairie provinces and the snowcapped peaks that pierced the porcelain blue of the western skies.

Even with the beauty of the landscape before him, Frank's thoughts were centered on Ann, and he wrote about "something that grips me here in Sidney!" He knew, however, he could not stay in Sidney.

As he prepared to leave for the mud and filth of the trenches on the Western Front, Frank could only hope he might one day be able to follow his heart back to Sidney. Frank trusted God, but then again so did many other young men whose lives were not spared by the sinful and merciless acts of war.

Chapter 2
THE WINDS OF WAR

On *February 8, 1917*, Frank's battalion entrained for Halifax, Nova Scotia, where the troopship SS *Southland* waited to take them to England. Frank wrote enthusiastically to Ann concerning his adventures on the North Atlantic. With time to contemplate what the future might hold for him, he quoted these lines from "The Wiser Prayer" by Isaac Ogden Rankin:

> *Once in earth's storms I asked for sheltering care,*
> *For warmth of fire, the shelter of a roof.*
> *Now, Lord, I bring a more discerning prayer—*
> *Make my heart weatherproof.*
> *Enough of folly and enough of fear!*
> *Forgive, O Lord, the weak prayers I have prayed.*
> *Through storm and strife, O keep my courage clear,*
> *My fixed heart undismayed.*

Europe

Encamped along the Thames River in England, Frank worried about Ann. He had not received a single letter for over two weeks. Later, he discovered that a torpedo had sunk the SS *Tacoma*, bearing Canadian mail, at the very spot the SS *Southland* had avoided by changing course. More than ever, Frank was now aware he might not see Ann again. Nevertheless, when Ann's letters did make it through, his hope for their reunion grew stronger and stronger.

By mid-May, the 47th Battalion crossed the Channel to France. Still, the war seemed far away. Everywhere one looked, apple and pear blossoms emblazoned the spring countryside. Frank particularly enjoyed visiting quaint villages and watching the vibrant French children at play.

Camp life, however, was a stark contrast to the ideal scenery. Without complaining, Frank described crowded tents and a lack of privacy. During the day, they marched for miles with heavy packs to toughen up for the rigors of trench warfare. At night, they polished brass and prepared their gear for combat. Sometimes the battalion band played songs such as "My Wild Irish Rose," "I Feel So Lonely," "Sweet Genevieve," "Bonnie Dundee," and "I Want to Go Home!" Frank commented, "So do I!"

In letters to Ann, Frank suggested the rigors of military life were a part of God's will. He wrote, "I believe He wants me to be a missionary. I believe all my life will be more or less of a camping-out like this. I sometimes wonder what I am going to do when I get back to Canada. If God permits, I am going to the foreign field." The testimony of a friend who had gone as a missionary to Taiwan (then called Formosa) and a book written by another missionary to Taiwan later stirred Frank's interest in China.

In August 1917, the 47th Battalion left their pleasant surroundings and moved into the trenches of northern France. There, the men awaited orders to go "over the top" in what history would remember as the Battle of Lens. Before dawn, Frank's unit huddled in their trenches and covered their ears while artillery fire bombarded enemy positions. Then, as first light creased the eastern sky, Canadian soldiers raced into battle with fixed bayonets amid bursting artillery shells, the staccato firing of machine guns, and the acrid smell of burning cordite. Frank, with other stretcher bearers, followed close behind.

Suddenly, an artillery shell exploded in front of the stretcher bearers. A piece of shrapnel ripped through Frank's helmet, the impact fracturing his skull. As his comrades swept on, Frank was left behind in no-man's-land with a paralyzed right leg. His partner was dead. They had been in action for less than five minutes.

With daylight approaching, Frank lay quietly, feigning death, as enemy lines were near, and bullets were whistling by overhead. He remained there all day until, under cover of darkness, he crawled back to his own lines, dragging his paralyzed leg.

Following treatment in a field hospital, the medics transferred Frank to No. 22 General Hospital on the Channel coast. A letter to Ann proclaimed, "I am in one of the best hospitals in France. My doctor is a very famous head specialist." (His "head specialist" was the noted Dr. Foster Kennedy, a pioneer neurosurgeon with the Harvard Medical Unit.)

When Frank showed he could bend his right knee, Dr. Kennedy indicated he would walk again. Frank wrote, "Praise God," but admitted it might take a year. Dr. Kennedy later inserted a silver plate in Frank's skull, replacing the fractured bone.

Ann's letters, full of sympathy, bore dried maple

leaves to remind Frank of Canada. Lying in a hospital bed, Frank thought about Ann and their future together. His nasty wound had taken him out of the war, probably sparing his life. Through all of this, he continually thanked God for His gracious extension of the gift of life. But then it dawned on Frank—if God had spared his life, He must have something in mind for his and Ann's future.

Chapter 3
THE WILL OF GOD

A fter a short hospital stay in England, Frank sailed for Canada. He again wrote to Ann, suggesting he should go to China, perhaps under the auspices of the Church of the Nazarene. He explained that the pay of a Nazarene minister is very small and later wrote: "There is the holy joy of being able to speak the truth unfettered. There are so many blessings in the Bible promised to the poor—this is to Christ's poor."

Ann responded, "You hurt me a little when you mentioned your poverty. I hope you do not think it would affect our friendship in any way. I do not know what wealth is, but I do know a little of poverty."

Frank stayed in eastern Canada until May 15, 1918, accepting a temporary post as classics master at the High School for Boys in Quebec City. He anticipated ordination at the district assembly in Portland, Oregon.

Ann asked, "Why ordination in the Nazarene church?"

Frank replied,

Brother Dave [Phillips] and I joined the little [Nazarene] church in Victoria before going overseas. I know you simply couldn't help liking them if you met them. The ministers are not paid very much, but the reward comes in being able to live very near to the lives of those who have a struggle, in being able to sympathize with them, in seeing souls saved and real spiritual work. The church has strict rules against theaters, playing cards, wearing of jewelry, and fine clothes, belonging to secret societies like Masons and Orangemen [militant Protestants in Northern Ireland]. None of these rules do I find irksome.

On his way to Portland, Frank spent a week with Ann in Sidney. On a morning hike up Mount Newton, they stopped by a fallen log under a giant fir tree. Kneeling together, they betrothed themselves to each other and dedicated their lives to God's work without reservation.

Frank continued his journey to Portland and wrote about the 1918 District Convention:

> There are about 300 people. The singing fairly lifts you off your feet. All this morning there is a great debate about dividing the district into two, as it is getting too large. Such speaking! Best of all is the remarkable feeling. There was not a single hard word, and everybody was in great good humor. They were just seeking to know what was right in the matter. That is holiness. They are not in the least fanatical. So loving and friendly. I never heard so many good speakers in all my life before. Bro. Little introduced me to General Superintendent Mr. Goodwin, who then introduced me to the assembly. All stood up and clapped and cheered. Since then people are rushing up to me all the time and wanting to hear about the war.

Rev. Little urged Frank, now an ordained Nazarene minister, to join him in evangelistic meetings throughout the Pacific Northwest. Dressed in a Canadian army uniform and relating his war experiences, Frank attracted many who were eager to hear news from the Western Front. Many who came to see and hear Frank also found salvation under the preaching of Rev. Little.

During this travel period, Dr. Olive M. Winchester, vice president of Northwest Nazarene College (NNC), heard that Frank held a master's degree from McGill. She began talking to Frank about a teaching position. Nevertheless, Frank remained convinced that God's will for his life involved China. If NNC was part of his future, God would have to make it clear.

Chapter 4
A SAGEBRUSH COLLEGE

T hinking of foreign missionary service, that year
(1918) Frank urged Ann to enroll either at Pasadena (Nazarene) College (now Point Loma Nazarene
University) in Pasadena, California, or Northwest
Nazarene College in Nampa, Idaho. Ann decided to
attend NNC, as it was much closer to home. Frank
helped persuade Ann, saying, "President Orton Wiley is one of the finest educators in the West!" (H.
Orton Wiley was president of NNC at that time.)

Soon afterward, Frank received an offer from
NNC for a professorship in modern languages. The
job included a salary of $750 for 10 months. Sudden-
ly, it seemed God's will for Frank and Ann was big-
ger and more dynamic than anything they had previously imagined.

In addition to the college, its academy, and
grammar school, another Nazarene institution had
also taken root in Nampa. Dr. and Mrs. T. E. Mangum's vision for establishing a hospital and nurses'
school to train medical missionaries for foreign fields
had led to the founding of Samaritan Hospital and
School of Nursing. The hospital and nursing school
were located across the street from the college,
where they stood until phased out in 1957.

With a teaching position in Nampa, Frank and Ann were married in a private home in Oregon City, Oregon, on September 16, 1918. Rev. Charles E. Ketler, pastor of the local Nazarene church, officiated, and Ann wore a brown traveling suit, as they were departing for Nampa later that evening.

With the opening of the fall term in 1919, Ann enrolled in a medical course taught by Dr. Mangum. She also took courses in Bible and piano. But before the second term began, Ann's mother died. With a sense of responsibility, Ann traveled back to Sidney to help her father care for her younger brothers and sisters.

Frank wrote often with news from Nampa. President Wiley extended his teaching contract for another year, and the General Board of Foreign Missions in Kansas City tentatively assigned Frank and Ann to China.

By May 1920, Ann's father found a housekeeper, and Ann returned to Nampa. She and Frank spent the summer visiting churches throughout the Northwest and western Canada, talking about China and God's call to that ancient land.

A few months later Frank wrote in his diary: "The year with its possibilities lies ahead of us. What eternities lie hidden in it?"

They were soon to find out.

Chapter 5
CHINA, THE FIRST TERM

On October 28, 1920, Frank and Ann Sutherland sailed from Vancouver, British Columbia, on a Japanese steamer called the SS *Fushimi Maru*. The A. J. Smiths were also sailing for China, and the Prescott Bealses, bound for the Nazarene work in India, were on board as well. Frank wrote in his diary of being blessed on reading from Josh. 1:7: "Be strong and very courageous. Be careful to obey all the law my servant Moses gave you; do not turn from it to the right or to the left, that you may be successful wherever you go." And then, in verse 9, "Have I not commanded you? Be strong and courageous. Do not be terrified; do not be discouraged, for the LORD your God will be with you wherever you go."

When the group arrived in Tientsin,[1] China, they contacted Rev. and Mrs. L. C. Osborn. With the Osborns leading the way, the missionaries traveled by rickshaw and train to attend the Peking Foreign Language School. Here they joined Rev. and Mrs. Harry Wiese and Dr. and Mrs. R. G. Fitz.

---

1. A Pronunciation Guide is provided on page 94 for Chinese and other unfamiliar words.

The new missionaries now saw the real China for the first time. Beggars abounded, graves dotted the countryside, and mud-walled villages followed each other in monotonous procession. Nevertheless, they would soon fall in love with the vibrant and energetic Chinese people, who were always full of good humor despite living in such bleak poverty.

With 7,000 individual characters required just to read a newspaper, learning Chinese was a cumbersome but vital task. Knowing the language was essential for missionaries hoping to win Chinese men and women for Jesus. Frank's diary records, "What a mountain of difficulty this language is!"

Under the comity agreements among the various Protestant missionary groups in China, the Church of the Nazarene's territorial assignment included several counties in the far west of the Shantung Province. Later, the Nazarenes acquired another five counties in the adjacent Hopei Province—counties also shared by the Mennonites.

Two million Chinese people lived in these counties. They would hear the gospel only if Nazarenes and Mennonites brought it to them. Both denominations established their mission headquarters in Taming (formerly Tamingfu), a walled city with a population of about 40,000.

Language school closed in mid-June. The Wieses, Fitzes, and Sutherlands all went to the mountains of the Honan Province to escape the humidity and rains that plague the North China plains in July and August. Other missionaries already in China, besides the Osborns, included Rev. and Mrs. Peter Kiehn, Rev. and Mrs. O. P. Deale, and Miss Pearl Denbo.

During this period, many Chinese people mistrusted foreigners, sometimes calling them "foreign devils." They still remembered the Boxer Rebellion of 1899—1900, in which militant Chinese were fanatically antiforeign. More than anything else, they resented the British imposition of the opium trade on China. Calling themselves the "righteous harmonious fists," they struck out at all foreigners. In turn, Westerners called them "Boxers."

Early missionaries broke down much of this prejudice through compassionate ministries, including the medical clinic in Taming. The medical ministry fell under the direction of Dr. Fitz, and a few years later, the clinic developed into the three-storied, 100-bed Bresee Memorial Hospital. At that time, the hospital was one of the largest medical facilities in rural North China. In the 15 or 16 years of its operation, Chinese patients came from southern Hopei and western Shantung Provinces with cataracts, tumors, injuries, and various sicknesses.

In 1920-21 the rains ceased, and North China languished under famine. Chinese with bloated stomachs ate dried leaves, roots, bark, and ground-up corncobs, which, as Rev. L. C. Osborn commented, only extended their misery a few days. Missionary groups operating in China rallied to stop the starvation. Overseas Nazarenes contributed $25,000 to a famine relief fund that enabled the missionaries to go from house to house distributing food. During this time, it took only three cents a day to feed each of the Chinese.

These compassionate ministries, however, caused many people to wonder if the so-called rice

Christians would disappear after the food distributions stopped. To the contrary, the church in China continued long after the missionaries returned home —a fitting testimony to the authenticity of many Chinese conversions.

* * *

Nazarene missionaries worked in a China undergoing transition. The last of the Manchu emperors fell in 1912, and control of North China passed to provincial leaders. These leaders were called warlords because they often commanded armies, some of which roved about collecting taxes and making life miserable for people. Other armies that were actually huge robber bands owed allegiance to no one except themselves. This forced the Chinese to remain inside walled cities at night.

Sun Yat-sen's central government of the new Chinese Republic lay far to the south along the Yangtze River. Generalissimo Chiang Kai-shek united China in 1928 but lacked effective power in North China, which remained under the control of the warlords.

* * *

For Frank and Ann, their chain of command began with the China Mission Council. Leaders were elected to the council from among the missionaries themselves. This council assigned Frank and Ann to Chengan (formerly Ch'eng An), a poor city with walls of adobe brick plastered with straw and mud.

On November 30, 1921, Frank and Ann traveled to Chengan, where they set up a temporary headquarters and held services with a Chinese evangelist.

Thirty Chinese attended the first Sunday morning service, and 43 showed up in the afternoon. As word about the foreigners spread, even more people came, totaling 200 on Christmas Day. When Frank's language skills improved, he, too, began preaching.

No foreigners had ever lived in Chengan. On completion of their house, Frank and Ann thought it might help to let a group of women see it. One woman carefully lifted the lid of every box, as she had been told that the powerful medicines of the Westerners came from pickling Chinese babies! Ann overheard her tell the other women, "Now I know it is not true."

Ann worked with Chinese women, who led lives of hard and unremitting toil. Adding to their burden, elders bound female feet during ages 5 through 12. Long strips of cloth were wrapped around each foot, folding the small toes underneath and forcing the foot into a wedge shape. They pulled the cloth bindings tighter and tighter until the foot conformed. What started as a mark of gentility and beauty for courtesans of the Imperial Court back in the Sung Dynasty (A.D. 960—1279) became a requirement for brides all over China. The new Chinese Republic banned foot binding in 1912, but it continued for years in rural North China. Ann ministered to numerous women with bound feet.

In December 1922, General Superintendent Hiram F. Reynolds visited Chengan. Chinese from Chengan and the surrounding villages came to hear the distinguished visitor. Frank reported on Saturday's services: "A great day. Services in the A.M. to a packed house. Dr. Reynolds preached on the Holy

THE CHURCH OF THE NAZARENE IN CHENGAN, CHINA

ANN (FRONT RIGHT) WITH A GROUP OF WOMEN
AT THE CHENGAN CHURCH.

Spirit, emphasizing purity rather than power to correct some wrong ideas. He preached with great fire. There were about 60 seekers. The coming of Dr. and Mrs. Reynolds has been a great blessing to us. Not only have there been many seekers and finders, but our own vision has been clarified and strengthened."

The China Mission Council, which assigned Frank and Ann to Chengan, decided to start a Bible school in Taming. The school would be training Chinese as pastors and leaders. Due to his experience in education, they chose Frank as its leader.

Frank and Ann accepted the assignment, leaving their home in Chengan to move to Taming. The Bible school opened with 10 students the day after Frank and Ann's arrival. Frank still served the church in Chengan on weekends, traveling on dirt roads by bicycle, rickshaw, and foot.

The next summer, with the close of Bible school, Frank visited Chengan. While holding a service, he asked for testimonies. To his delight, several of the returning Bible school students responded. The simplicity and naturalness of their testimonies impressed him, and he wrote, "This meeting will bear fruit in the future."

✳   ✳   ✳

Fighting in and about Taming broke out and increased as the autumn of 1925 approached. The northern army under Jong Tso Lin, a warlord who controlled Manchuria and much of North China, turned over control of all but Manchuria to Chiang Kai-shek and his Nationalists. A Nationalist army under Fen Yu Hsiang came to replace them.

Several days elapsed between this "changing of the guards," during which a radical antiforeign group attempted to break into the city. About 30 members slipped in before the gates were locked. As a warning, the city police beheaded two of the bandits and hung their heads above the city gates. (Both the Nazarene and Mennonite walled compounds were outside the walls of Taming and thus outside the city's protection.)

Through all of this, Frank continued his travels to Chengan. Infantry training in Canada and England had strengthened his body for the rigors of bicycling. Ann never complained when left alone, whether in Taming with other missionaries or by herself in Chengan. During lonely nights, when unknown dangers lurked in the bandit-infested countryside, the commitment they made to each other and to God held her steady.

Once, upon returning at night to Chengan from holding services in Nanlo, Frank found the city gates locked. A cooperative guard, although unwilling to open the gate, lowered a rope and pulled him, apostle Paul fashion, up and over the wall!

Unrest continued as warlords vied for territory and the central government sought to extend its control. Antiforeign feelings were returning, fanned by radicals from the Boxer movement and an emergent Communism.

Frank and Ann had now served six years. The Mission Council and Nazarene Headquarters in Kansas City recommended and approved furloughs for the Sutherlands and the Wieses. Ten years would elapse before they would see China again.

Chapter 6
RETURN TO NAMPA

While in China, Ann had given birth to three sons, John Campbell, David Hollingsworth, and Robert Bowman. The Sutherlands, now five, sailed from Shanghai in April 1926, on Canadian Pacific's SS *Empress of Australia.*

After a few pleasant days in Quebec, the family returned to Nampa, and Frank once again became Prof. F. C. Sutherland. The family rented a house from the Harper family about two city blocks from the NNC campus. (Dr. Albert Harper, one of the Harpers' sons, would later serve as editor in chief of Sunday School publications in Kansas City.) Other Nazarenes lived nearby, and as everyone survived on minimal wages, they frequently helped one another with garden produce and eggs.

In 1927 Ann gave birth to Edith Margaret, the first Sutherland born on American soil. Born at Samaritan Hospital, Margaret would eventually train there as a nurse.

In 1929 the Wieses and the Fitzes returned to China. Civil war still raged in North China, but conditions in the Taming area seemed to have stabilized, warranting their return. The Department of Foreign Missions, however, lacked sufficient funds to send the Sutherlands and their many children. Dr. Russell V. DeLong, NNC's president in 1929, offered Frank the chair of the Department of History at $150 per month. Frank accepted, and the Sutherlands remained at NNC until the door opened for the family to return to China.

On October 17, 1929, the stock market crashed. Soon the United States, along with the rest of the world, entered into the Great Depression. Educational budgets suffered, and NNC cut Frank's salary for the 1931-32 school year to $50 a month. The college would pay more if and when they received additional money. According to a letter of intent from the Board of Regents, unpaid salary at the end of the school year would not be "debt owed by the college."

There were benefits, however, as loyal Nazarenes rallied to support their college. NNC adopted a transfer system, through which students from farms could bring in produce instead of cash. In turn, some of this produce was given to faculty to offset salary.

In addition, students worked for faculty to reduce the total amount of tuition owed. Some students also worked to ease Ann's task of caring for her large family. Francis Charles was born in 1928, Paul William arrived in 1931, and Ellen Ann in 1933, totaling seven children in all.

Although NNC faced financial troubles during the depression in the '30s, the students and faculty had faith in God as they dealt with these problems, remembering that He had delivered them from a desperate financial problem just a few years earlier. In 1927 NNC had a debt of $93,000 and teetered on the brink of receivership. President Russell V. De-Long, newly inaugurated, faced the problem aggressively by launching a campaign to pay the debt. A bonded treasurer held all donated moneys in trust until the entire $93,000 was secured. November 1, 1928, became the zero hour. If the amount on hand was less than $93,000 on November 1, all money would be returned to donors and the college lost.

Dr. DeLong pled with 6,000 Nazarenes across the zone to give sacrificially. Ranchers mortgaged lands, and faculty members pledged from past and future salaries; but in the spring of 1928 they still lacked $15,000. They had approached every church on the region and didn't know where to turn for more cash.

Prayer and fasting accompanied the campaign from its onset. Every Friday night at 10:00, faculty and students gathered to pray, often until 2:00 or 3:00 in the morning.

Nevertheless, in early fall 1928, the college remained short of its goal.

In a last-minute effort, General Superintendent R. T. Williams appealed to NNC's constituency through the pages of its paper, the *Nazarene Messenger*. On October 24, business agent J. C. Henson pled with the churches, saying, "Friends of Christian education, please, please help us over the top." But in spite of their efforts, on Wednesday, October 31, NNC remained $5,000 short.

At prayer meeting that evening, students and faculty pledged $1,000. One student gave the 27 cents in his pocket, and another gave the $50 he was saving for the following semester's tuition. Telegrams went out that night to churches and friends. Suddenly, on November 1, replies came pouring in. Some came with money, others with encouragement. One Colorado man asked to know what they lacked and said he would pay it. By evening they had reached their goal.

Besides saving the college, this campaign provided an entire generation of NNC students with a great lesson in prayer, faith, and persistence. To this day, it is their greatest legacy from their years at NNC.

✳ ✳ ✳

All Nazarene colleges and universities schedule special revival services in the fall and spring. They are, in reality, evangelistic campaigns that contribute greatly to the spiritual life of a campus community. Many alumni look back on these times as defining moments in their lives, as every now and then there are special outpourings of the Holy Spirit.

Such a revival occurred in November 1931. Evangelist J. W. Montgomery gave a stirring message on the influence all lives have on others for good or for evil. Students who appeared hardened to the gospel began seeking out Christian friends for prayer. Soon spontaneous prayer meetings broke out, often preempting classes, meals, and everything else on campus. Students walked about the dining hall with hands uplifted, while others shouted. Many students settled God's call to the ministry or to the mission field during these special services. Earl Mosteller of the Cape Verde Islands, Brazil, Portugal, and the Azores, and Louise (Robinson) Chapman of Africa were among those who committed their lives during NNC's revivals.

About this time, the depression deepened, and alternative income was necessary. Frank used the photography skills honed in his father's pharmacy to earn extra money during the summer, and a Nazarene fruit grower in Emmett, Idaho, hired Prof. Kent Goodnow and Frank to pick apples. Their pay included cull apples sufficient to fill a large storage bin in the Sutherlands' basement.

Frank's father urged him to go on for a Ph.D. and offered financial assistance. Dr. Reuben Gilmore, then NNC's president, supported the idea, as NNC had so few faculty members with doctorates. Frank chose the University of Washington, and Ann, sensing this as God's will, agreed to his being in Seattle during the summers of 1934 and 1935.

Then, in 1936, China's door suddenly reopened for the Sutherlands. However, it opened into an uncertain future. Japan had conquered Manchuria. Would China be next?

Chapter 7
AN OPEN DOOR

Wars raged everywhere in 1936. Mussolini annexed Ethiopia, Hitler moved troops into the Rhineland, and the Spanish Civil War began. Japan was pressuring China for special privileges and political control in several northern provinces. War clouds hung over the rest of China as well.

Inside China, however, the political climate favored the spread of the gospel. These exhilarating days owed a great deal to the leadership of the revolutionary Sun Yat-sen and his New China Republic. Sun had married into the Soong family, who were all staunch Methodists. The youngest Soong daughter, Mei-ling, married President Chiang Kai-shek who, in turn, also embraced Christianity. Her brother, T. V. Soong, ranked second to President Chiang in the Nationalist government.

The China missionaries, full of optimism, requested Nazarene Mission Headquarters to send the Sutherlands. They wanted Frank to reopen the Bible school. The Department of Foreign Missions agreed but stipulated that John and David, soon to enter college, should remain in the States.

Along with the Sutherlands, the families of Rev. John Pattee, Rev. Geoffrey Royall, and Miss Rhoda Schurman converged on Seattle. In the depths of the Great Depression, the sending of this large group of

THE SUTHERLANDS IN CHINA (LEFT TO RIGHT):
ELLEN, FRANCIS, FRANK, ROBERT, ANN, MARGARET, AND PAUL.

Nazarene missionaries was a tremendous expression of faith by Nazarene Mission Headquarters.

✳   ✳   ✳

The SS *Choku Maru* slipped over the sandbar at the mouth of the Hai Ho River and docked at Ta Ku, the dirty, noisy, and smelly port city for Tientsin. Coolies swarmed over the ship to unload baggage and cargo. They slid trunks down a smooth plank from the ship's deck to the dock, where Ann watched in horror as one trunk gained too much speed and split open, spilling its contents at the bottom. With relief, she watched as their trunks arrived safely on the ground.

By the time all the Sutherland trunks and barrels were ashore to be shipped down the Grand Canal to Taming, it was past noon, and everyone was hungry. A restaurant in the railroad station offered Western food "of a sort." Frank ordered scrambled egg sandwiches for the whole family.

The Chinese of that time did not refrigerate eggs and paid little attention to age. They considered fresh eggs tasteless. To top things off, it was hot, and wind was kicking up street dust. Flies swarmed around the Sutherlands' heads, and their stomachs churned from the pungent smells of raw China. Because of their previous term in China, Frank and Ann knew that a person adjusts after a year or so. The children, on the other hand, were in shock!

Soon everyone sat down on wooden seats. Traveling third class by railway, the Sutherlands watched as they rolled by the flatland of North China. Junks, sampans, and an occasional tugboat on the nearby Hai Ho River seemed to float on the fields. At Tientsin, the missionaries separated. The Pattees and Royalls went to Peking for language study, and the Sutherlands and Miss Schurman continued on by train to Hantan, the railhead for Taming. (Miss Schurman had come to China to help teach the missionary children.)

Rev. Harry Wiese and Dr. Henry Wesche met the Sutherlands and Miss Schurman in Hantan with their cars, an open Chevrolet of about 1927 vintage and a 1930 Dodge sedan. They tied what luggage they could on the fenders and transported the rest to Taming by cart.

Nazarene missionaries in China were about to enter a few golden years of reaping in fields that were "white already to harvest" (John 4:35, KJV). Never before had any one period presented such opportunities to win Chinese for Jesus. And no one could be certain how long the door would remain open.

Frank and Ann eagerly anticipated seeing their Chinese friends and missionaries to whom they had said "Good-bye" 10 years earlier. Ann, writing to John and David, described their first visit back to Chengan:

> We have only visited Chengan for a day and night since we returned. We hear on all sides of us, "Why, isn't that Pastor Sutherland who used to live here and who has been gone these 8 to 10 years? And isn't that his wife? And I wonder if any of these children are the three they had when they were here!" One dear old Christian woman that I used to know took my hands and stroked them and said with tears trickling down her cheek, "Oh, you don't know how we missed you and longed for you and prayed all these years for the Lord to send you back. Now He has answered my prayers, and here you are!" We were greeted by shopkeepers and men of the town all along the way to our old place of worship with "Welcome back, welcome back."

Reunions like this have always encouraged missionaries. But Frank and Ann were thinking more soberly about the future of the work. The recent war in Manchuria and the saber rattling by Japanese militants left no doubt in their minds that time was short.

More than anything else, all of the missionaries knew the extreme importance of training Chinese pastors and leaders for service. Reopening the Bible school would allow the Church of the Nazarene to continue growing in China long after the missionaries evacuated.

Chapter 8
THE GOLDEN YEARS

With the central government of Chiang Kai-shek controlling most of China, the country was relatively calm. Universal education held top priority, and new normal schools had sprung up to educate teachers. Consequently, when Frank and Ann returned, the climate was friendly to missionaries.

In the 1930s, political stability and a friendly government provided a window of opportunity to evangelize the Chinese. Enthusiastic missionaries recognized an openness to the gospel unlike any they had previously seen. These were the golden years of missionary service in China. The emerging Communists, still confined to the western provinces, seemed to be the only potential obstacle to the work.

Missionaries already at the hospital in Taming included Miss Mary Pannell, superintendent of nurses; Miss Catherine Flagler, the hospital treasurer; Dr. Wesche; his wife, Mabel; and their daughter, Mary. Other missionaries included Rev. Wiese; his wife, Catherine; and their children, Florence, Pauline, Clarence, and James. Finally, Miss Ida Vieg, a women's worker, completed the eager group that seized this unprecedented opportunity.

The Sutherlands moved into a large, three-story brick house. The home was built during the famine when labor was plentiful and grain was the pay. A kitchen, pantry, serving room, vegetable preparation room, dining and living rooms, and two studies made up the first floor. Ann used one study to teach elderly, illiterate Chinese women a simplified phonetic script that enabled them to read the Bible. She also wrote letters, prepared orders, and operated a mimeograph machine in this room. Frank took the other study as his office for administering the Bible school. Four bedrooms and a sewing room made up the second floor, and three storage rooms made up the third floor.

The Bible school opened with bright young students, including both males and females. The missionaries placed a high priority on education and training—a priority later validated in the turbulent years after the missionaries had left China. Chinese men and women trained at the Bible school would effectively lead the church during those perilous days.

Frank described a typical day in the life of the Bible school in *Distinctive Days*, the correlated missionary study book for 1943-44, edited by Edith P. Goodnow (Nazarene Publishing House):

At six o'clock in the morning, while it is still dark, a student slips out of his bed, hastily dons his long winter garment of padded cotton, and hurries out into the yard where he rings the large bell. Soon dim little oil lamps with narrow wicks are lit in each room, where three or four students sleep in double-decker cots with only a small space between them. Even before the rising bell one can often hear the voice of prayer as some have gone into corners of the school yard to find a place to pray.

From the cook house rises a cloud of smoke, and one hears the click clack of the bellows as the cook's helper fans the fire that is cooking the millet for the morning meal, or steaming the bread, which should be hot as it reaches the tables. Soon a long line of students pours out of the dormitory door nearest to the cook house. They are going, each one with a little enamelware basin in their hands, for warm water to wash their faces and hands. Then there is quiet till seven o'clock, except for the voice of prayer and the click clack of the fire blower in

THE BIBLE SCHOOL IN TAMING

the cook house. The students are all at their private devotions. One morning the dean of men came in with a shining face. "I've walked the length of the corridors," he said, "and in every room there were open Bibles on the tables and men on their knees on the floor."

At seven o'clock, both male and female students ate breakfast in separate dining rooms, attended chapel service, and then spent the rest of the day in classes. On Sundays, Bible school students cycled out to villages for evangelization. Riding bicycles, Frank and Ann led groups of men and women on these trips. Their bicycles were festooned with gospel banners.

The Bible school overflowed with students, the Bresee Memorial Hospital treated and evangelized patients, and work at the outstation churches continued at a fast pace during these glorious years. Nevertheless, missionaries knew that a climate so amiable to the gospel might not last. Jesus said, "As long as it is day, we must do the work of him who sent me. Night is coming, when no one can work" (John 9:4).

With this in mind, they worked with a sense of urgency. Many signs suggested night was fast approaching. And while they could not possibly have imagined how difficult things would get, they were making sure there would always be a flicker of light in the darkness.

Chapter 9
FLOODS AND WAR

In July 1937, Japanese troops maneuvering near the Marco Polo Bridge just south of Peking requested entrance to a nearby village. Apparently, the troops wanted to search for two or three missing soldiers. Village officials denied their request. In response, the Japanese opened fire, and the war that began in Manchuria now came to China.

Later that summer, Peking[2] fell, and the Japanese advanced along the Hankow Railway. This railway passed through part of the Nazarene field in Hantan. Once Hantan fell, the Japanese would come to Taming, the headquarters for the Chinese army in the southern Hopei Province. Nazarene missionaries, now in the path of war, listened for news as Japanese soldiers continued their relentless advance down the railway toward Hantan.

By telegram and letter, the American Embassy advised all missionaries in the area to leave China. Every Nazarene missionary lived in Taming except for the Royalls and Pattees, who were still in language

---

2. Also known as Peiping; today the capital city of Beijing.

study in Peking. But before war came to Taming, North China went through a great natural tragedy.

* * *

North China always welcomes rain. This time, however, it continued to rain day after day. Puddles became ponds, and soon water covered the whole countryside. For a while, the children had great fun sailing toy boats and building mud dikes and dams. Then the nearby Wei River burst its dikes, and flood-waters approached Taming. At least for the moment, the solid wall around the mission compound provided an effective barrier for the compound itself. The hospital, on the other hand, stood outside the compound wall near Taming's north gate. Workers hastily built dikes to save the hospital's lower floor.

The mud houses of the Chinese collapsed into the floodwaters, leaving families huddled on high ground. Homeless, they constructed mat huts, hoping to dry out their meager possessions. The missionaries found a stranded Christian family and brought them into the mission compound with all their salvageable possessions.

Despite the wall around the mission compound, the rising waters found their way inside, and the basements began to flood. Rev. Wiese tried unsuccessfully to evacuate the basements with an old gasoline-powered pump.

By September, floodwaters receded, and the land dried sufficiently for the Japanese advance to continue. Hantan finally fell, and the Japanese turned toward Taming. A road built by the American Red Cross to bring grain to starving Chinese in Taming during the famine of the 1920s now brought destruction. More telegrams arrived from the American Embassy, all with the same message: "Get out!"

The missionaries met often and discussed what to do. (Today, World Mission Division would not allow missionaries to remain in an area against the wishes of the United States Embassy.) The work was continuing to prosper among the receptive Chinese. Could they simply walk away from working while there was still daylight?

Hours upon hours were spent in prayer, as everyone listened for "higher orders." They worried about the Bible school buildings, the Bresee Memorial Hospital, and the large tabernacle-type church at Taming. What would become of all these during the upcoming battles? More importantly, would walking out seem like abandonment to the faithful Chinese Christians? On the other hand, what could the missionaries do to protect themselves? The missionaries struggled with these difficult decisions as they met and prayed together through long, sleepless nights.

Soon, Japanese planes appeared over Taming. At first, they simply circled about, but city officials warned the people to avoid crowds and to scurry for cover when the planes were in sight.

Although the Sutherlands held Canadian passports, they joined the rest of the missionaries in displaying American flags. Rev. Wiese arranged for five large flags to be painted on reed mats, and they displayed a few cloth ones as well.

The missionaries dug trenches to provide additional safety during air raids. But after the families had dug down about three feet, the summer rains left a high water table, which filled the trenches with water. This forced them to settle for shallow, foxhole-style trenches. During air raids, everyone knelt in foxholes and kept their heads down.

The city of Taming conducted compulsory air-raid drills. A watchman stood on the city wall and repeatedly struck a large bell when the planes were approaching. At the mission compound, Rev. Wiese fastened a battery-powered horn to a high pole. At his signal, everyone raced for the trenches. Three slow honks signaled it was safe to come out. The initial drill went nicely, as a lone plane flew overhead without dropping any bombs.

The first real attack came on a Sunday morning when everyone was scattered around the compound. Frank was in bed with a cold, Mrs. Wiese was on her way into Taming, and the rest of the missionaries were in the worship service. All of the missionary children were in Sunday School.

A plane circled at a low altitude over the city before dropping five bombs on an airfield less than a mile away from the compound. Mr. Yu, superintendent of the Sunday School, asked, "Suppose a bomb had fallen from that airplane right through this roof. What do you think would have happened?"

An elderly Chinese lady quickly responded, "Jesus would have put out His hand and caught it!"

Sadly, future events tested this simple, trusting faith. One morning, while those on the compound were eating breakfast, a young Chinese man burst in and announced the arrival of three planes. Everyone rushed out to see not three, but six two-man, single-engine, low-wing, light bombers with the rising sun emblem clearly visible on their fuselages. The people in the compound ran for a spot near the wall and crouched in the shallow trenches.

For 20 minutes the planes, with engines roaring, crossed and recrossed, dive-bombing the airport, normal school, and nearby army camp. Frank, who had managed to grab a camera, stepped out of the trench into the open to get a shot of a plane just over the Wiese house. He responded promptly to Ann's "Frank, get back quickly before you get hit!"—but not before he got a picture!

After that morning, the missionaries felt the increasing pressure to leave. Chinese were fleeing Taming. Should the missionaries go as well? Should any of them stay? Leaderless soldiers and robber bands were already looting around Taming.

The missionaries discussed plans long into the night. The Chinese still held the port city of Tsingtao, where British and American warships were anchored. Tsingtao was a potentially safe haven for everyone.

Dr. Feng, the Chinese physician at the hospital, wanted to take his family to his wife's home. The house was located in a village near Tsingtao. Frank closed the Bible school, as he could no longer guarantee the safety of the students. With the departure of Dr. Feng, Dr. Hayne, and nurse Pannell, the hospital would carry on as a clinic with Chinese nurses and technicians.

Finally, they reached a decision. Missionary women and children left under the leadership of Frank and Dr. Feng. Mrs. Wiese, in agony over the thought of leaving her husband alone, decided to stay with their children. Besides the Sutherland and Feng families, others going included Dr. Hayne, Miss Flagler, nurse Pannell, a teacher returning to Tientsin, three Chinese personnel from the hospital, a Bible school couple and their child, and over 21 wheelbarrow men. Due to a sore foot, Miss Flagler could not walk. Rather than leaving her behind, they carried her on a makeshift sedan chair made by fastening poles to a kitchen chair.

The group left, anticipating three or four days of walking, a bus trip for about an hour or so, and an overnight train ride to Tsingtao. No one could have imagined the twists and turns the journey would take.

Chapter 10
FLIGHT FROM TAMING

I*n the predawn darkness* of October 13, 1937, everyone assembled in the mission compound. Some of the pole carriers and wheelbarrow men failed to show up, delaying the departure. Chinese pole carriers, so common even today and cheaper than wheelbarrow men, bear poles on their shoulders with baskets hung at each end. They walk steadily, matching their gait to the springing of the pole. An experienced pole carrier can even rotate the pole across his back to the opposite shoulder without missing a step.

The Chinese wheelbarrow has a large wheel with a narrow platform on each side. Lower than the axle, these platforms provide room for one or two people to sit or for goods. One man pulls and another pushes, gripping the widely spaced handles and having a strap across their shoulders to relieve some of the weight. The strength of these Chinese workers reflected lives of hard, physical labor. Ann often told stories about Chinese workers lifting heavy trunks by themselves—trunks that required two to four American stevedores to handle.

The tardy carriers did not appear. Soon, dawn would bring renewed bombing, catching the party near the city. They were forced to leave at once. After a tearful farewell with all the Wieses, the party walked out of the mission compound.

A wall and moat surrounded Taming with gates at the four compass points. With the north gate still closed for the night, they walked quietly around Taming's wall. By the time they reached the other side of the city, the South Gate was open. Here they joined a stream of Chinese going out into the countryside to escape the daytime air raids on Taming.

When the Chinese saw the missionaries were fellow refugees, Ann sensed bonds of sympathy with them. Looking back toward Taming, the missionary party saw Chinese soldiers in their gray uniforms atop the wall and the American flags flying over the Mennonite Mission.

Most pitiful among the Chinese hurrying out of Taming were the women with bound feet. Ann wrote of them: "Lily Feet, as bound feet were called, looked ludicrously out of place in this picture of Chinese womanhood fleeing before modern warfare. Husbands' and fathers' faces wore expressions of despair, almost of disgust, as they vainly begged them to 'hurry a little faster,' . . . so impossible on their crippled little feet."

The children, confined to the mission compound most of the summer, were now having great fun. They raced about, catching minnows in some of the roadside pools left over from the summer monsoons and looking for flowers.

Eventually the group reached the crossing at the Wei River, six miles south of Taming. They watched as thousands of Chinese soldiers in Chiang Kai-

ON THE MOAT SURROUNDING THE WALLS OF TAMING,
ANN WITH HER CHILDREN AND TWO OF THE WIESE CHILDREN.

shek's 29th Route Army crowded both banks, waiting for deployment to the north to defend Taming. A steam-powered tug, its stack belching black smoke, chugged back and forth across the Wei, moving men and supplies on barges.

In the distance, the group heard sounds of exploding shells and of airplanes strafing the road. This increased their anxiety to get away from the concentration of soldiers, but the ferryman delayed their crossing by demanding a high toll. Then, hearing the sound of another plane that seemed much closer, they all ran into the *koaliang* (broomcorn) fields and crouched, keeping their heads down. The plane found another target a mile or so away. Having reached an agreement on the toll, they were about to board the ferry when they heard yet another plane. Miss Flagler quickly hoisted a United States flag and then lowered it again as Chinese soldiers converged to crouch under its protection.

Once away from soldiers and refugees, all seemed normal except for the distant sound of bombs exploding in Taming. But their sense of safety evaporated when, along the way, Chinese told them of robbers and renegade soldiers roaming the area and preying on innocent civilians.

They reached Nanlo that evening. Even though there had been no time to send word ahead, they went immediately to the Mennonite Mission. Soldiers filled the city's inns and bought food and hot water faster than the shopkeepers could prepare the meals. Nevertheless, a resourceful Chinese brother in charge of the mission managed to feed the party. They slept soundly that night on wooden beds.

The next morning, the group was more cheerful, especially when they learned there were enough wheelbarrows available for everyone to ride. Little Ellen, riding on a wheelbarrow, started to sing "I'm H-A-P-P-Y"—a popular song at that time. Ann confessed that she more heartily joined in when Ellen later sang "Jesus Never Fails," "A Little Talk with Jesus," and "I Need Jesus."

The following night they reached the Nazarene outstation at Kwancheng (formerly Kwan Ch'eng) and enjoyed the fellowship of the Chinese pastor and his family. The town official, who was a Christian and friendly to the church, came to talk with Frank and Dr. Feng. He bore grim news, however, of a band of several hundred robbers operating in the area through which they planned to travel the next day. He offered an escort of 50 men, but with Miss Flagler's sedan chair plus such a large group of people, they would surely be viewed as an important provincial governor flanked by a personal escort. They committed their journey to the Lord in prayer and went to bed.

The next day, claiming the words from 1 Sam. 7:12, "Thus far has the LORD helped us," they set out

FRANK ENGAGED THESE MEN TO CARRY ELLEN AND PAUL, TOO TIRED TO WALK FARTHER, IN A BASKET.

to finish the trip alone. Around noon, they reached a dike holding back the floodwaters from an overflowing branch of the Yellow River. Climbing to the top of the dike, the missionary party looked out over a vast expanse of muddy and slow-moving water littered with *koaliang* stalks and tree branches. For thousands of years the Chinese have fought desperately to contain the Yellow River, so aptly named China's Sorrow. Throughout history, the river has overflowed dikes, which were built by laborers, flooding crops and devastating the homes of anyone living in the path of its fury.

The wheelbarrow men now raced along atop the dike in high spirits. From this point on they would not have to stop and ask for directions, and they would reach Fanshien about three or four miles farther along the dike.

A mile out of Fanshien, one of the Bible school students came bicycling toward them, his face beaming with happiness in seeing them again. When the group arrived in the city, they sent someone to find out about the bus to Tsinan (formerly Tsinanfu). The answer was shocking! The bus stopped running the week before. Hearing that some help might be available from Tsinan itself, they rushed off a telegram to a missionary friend. Only then did they take time to eat, feasting on millet soup and steamed bread. This diet, which had sustained them along the way, brought a new appreciation for the customary meal of rural North China.

On Sunday, they fellowshipped with Chinese Nazarenes in Fanshien. Following the afternoon service, they heard clanging from the north gate of Fanshien. The gate had been flung open to allow several carts to pass, rattling over the cobblestones, the horses at full gallop. Civil court officials (the yamen) in Fanshien were fleeing because a company of Chinese soldiers was coming to place the city under military rule.

Ann wondered why they were so afraid. She thought the court officials should welcome the weary and hungry soldiers who had been fighting battles for them. But the panic caused by this precipitous flight of the city fathers only increased when the news came that soldiers had entered the south gate and were looting the city.

As darkness fell on the leaderless city, the sounds of gates closing and bolts sliding into place traveled swiftly through the night air. And if there was not enough concern already, a wire from Tsinan announced that no transport would be available.

Ann wrote: "We were all rather agitated. I tried to calm myself and get the younger children to bed. They must have sensed the tenseness of the atmosphere, for their voices seemed shriller than usual, and their tongues chattered incessantly while I tried to strain my ears to hear what was going on outside. Mr. Sutherland was trying to hide our traveling money here and there about the room in unlikely places. He pinned a check inside his tie."

Nights in China during the late '30s were usually quiet except for the occasional barking of a dog or braying of a donkey. But this night was not an ordinary night in China. Ann listened as nearby dogs gave blood-curdling growls and barked furiously. She wondered when the soldiers might arrive. The mission gateman paced nervously back and forth and kept saying in Chinese, "Don't worry, it's all right."

The night passed uneventfully, and the missionaries sensed, once again, God's special protection. The next day, Frank and Dr. Feng went out seeking transport to Tsinan. They returned in triumph.

A man and his crew had concealed a boat in the muddy floodwaters. After a bit of bargaining, he agreed to take the party the 33 miles or so to where the floodwaters flowed into the main channel of the Yellow River. From there they could travel alongside the river to Tsinan. At Miss Pannell's suggestion, the group purchased several chickens for the trip and bid a fond farewell to the Fanshien Nazarenes. It would be the last time they would see Nazarenes on their trip.

The boat was about 35 feet long with a 10-foot beam. From the midsection the boat narrowed toward the squared-off bow and stern. Ribs, sheeted with heavy boards bent to contour, made up the hull, and a flat deck covered the entire boat. As the boat bobbed about three feet above the water, the travelers loaded their bedding rolls and suitcases onto the deck, using them as cushioned seats for the journey.

Now afloat on the floodwaters, they passed over submerged villages, trees, and *koaliang* fields. The boatmen used poles to accelerate their passage downstream, and they soon heard the roar of the Yellow River itself, now at flood stage.

The swift current suddenly swept them into the muddy, turbulent, rushing river that drains most of North China. At first, the boatmen lost control and

BARGING ON THE FLOODED PLAIN ON THEIR WAY TO THE YELLOW RIVER. MISS FLAGLER IS UNDER THE UMBRELLA, MISS PANNELL IS STANDING UP, AND DR. HAYNE IS FACING THE FLAG.

fought desperately to head the boat toward the bank. Hanging willow branches caught Miss Flagler's kitchen chair, almost sweeping her overboard. With great effort, the boatmen finally managed to tie the boat to the bank, and they spent the night on board. They were as far as the boatman had agreed to take them.

CARRYING MISS FLAGLER ACROSS A LOG PLACED OVER A STREAM

The next day, Frank and Dr. Feng went seeking another boat to take them downriver to Tsinan. They soon discovered that river traffic was limited to the military, which meant they would have to travel by foot along the Yellow River dike. If wheelbarrows or rickshaws were available, the missionary party would rent such to speed the journey along.

The group met many refugees crowding the dike on the north bank of the Yellow River, and as they went eastward, they encountered more and more soldiers. At one place they had to step aside to let 50 carts with guns and ammunition pass. Trenches and gun pits surrounded the dike itself, and although the Chinese soldiers were friendly, it seemed wise to cross over to the less crowded south bank.

Nearing the ferry crossing, the party heard the roar of rapids as the rushing, turbulent waters of the

Yellow River writhed and tossed about. The party was appalled to see little ferryboats, similar to the boat that bore them to Fanshien, pitching about in three- and four-feet waves. Ann wondered how the Chinese could possibly choose this site for a ferry crossing!

In spite of the turbulent waters, she remained calm. These men were part of generations of ferrymen and were experts at navigating floodwaters such as these. She sensed they were trustworthy.

Soon it was their turn to cross. They loaded baggage on one boat and boarded another. The ferrymen poled the boats upriver and then out into the current, which immediately swept them downstream. Using oars, they rowed furiously to cross to the far bank. Once in midstream, Miss Flagler once again narrowly escaped disaster, as a huge wave almost swept her into the turbulent waters. Eventually they entered still waters along the opposite bank and were poled upstream to a landing jetty.

Low hills border the south bank of the Yellow River, making the need for a dike unnecessary. But now their road followed the contour of the land, climbing and cresting with every hill, in sharp contrast to the flat roads typical of the dike along the opposite bank.

Fortunately, they obtained rickshaws and wheelbarrows, but some still had to walk due to the limited number available. The children, whose energies seemed boundless, enjoyed this immensely, but the adults struggled to walk up and down the hilly roads.

Later that evening, they came to a town surrounded by water. A Chinese Bible woman in charge of a large Presbyterian church gave them shelter for the night, and one of the town's officials, a Christian, promised to do what he could to help them. He sent word inquiring about boats going to Tsinan, but again, the boats were only carrying military personnel.

Then, after three long days of traveling by foot, they finally reached Tsinan. Ann wondered if ever an odder, dirtier-looking party ever rolled into a modern city on rickshaws and wheelbarrows under cover of night.

Frank, now broke, borrowed some money from a pharmacist friend of Dr. Feng who lived in Tsinan. Soon they experienced the luxury of train travel to Tsingtao. Ann wrote: "My emotions were almost running away with me. I felt like laughing and crying with joy and relief at being in a place of quiet and safety."

But while the missionaries thanked God for their escape, they were also keenly aware that the Chinese Christians in Taming were still under attack. From Tsingtao, they could only pray for the protection of the compound, for the sparing of lives, and ultimately for an end to the madness of war.

Chapter 11
COASTAL
INTERLUDE

The waters at Tsingtao were sparkling blue. The city itself sprawls over a hilly promontory on the shore of the Yellow Sea, far from the muddy outflow of the Yellow River. The Germans leased the land from the Chinese emperor in 1898 and built heavy fortifications in Tsingtao to defend their trading interests in the Orient. They also laid out a beautiful modern city with wide streets, parks, massive buildings of gray granite, and white stucco homes. All of this was in stark contrast to the bleak mud and gray brick houses of the villages in Taming.

The Sutherlands now enjoyed a peaceful time. The kids attended the American school for children of missionaries, diplomats, and businessmen. Frank and Ann, relieved of mission duties, spent time walking in parks, along ocean beaches, and exploring rocky points and old German fortifications with the children. Miss Flagler, in poor health and at retirement age after years of devoted service, sailed home from Tsingtao in November.

By December, the missionaries longed to join the Pattees, Royalls, and Miss Schurman, who had been isolated in Tientsin since war had swept over the Hopei Province. From there, they could return to

Taming and continue the work under the Japanese occupation. However, it was hard to book passage on a steamer from Tsingtao to Tientsin, as shipping companies, fearing a Japanese attack, kept many of their ships away from Tsingtao. Nevertheless, Frank finally secured tickets on a British ship set to sail later that month.

Ten days after they sailed for Tientsin, the Japanese occupied Tsingtao. Safe in Tientsin, the missionaries stayed at an old German mansion that later became the National Holiness Association Seminary. The mansion boasted two stories plus an attic, and the rooms all faced inward with balconies lining an open central area. Each family enjoyed a suite of rooms, and the balconies served as communal areas. In residence were the Pattees, Royalls, Miss Schurman, and now Dr. Hayne, Miss Mary Pannell, and the Sutherlands.

The Royalls and Pattees continued their language lessons, and fighting soon passed south of Taming. Frank, anxious to see the Wieses and the mission compound, left for Taming, wondering if there would be anything left.

Chapter 12

WORKING IN
OCCUPIED CHINA

The railroad, *now in Japanese hands*, ran only during daylight. Chinese guerrilla armies often blew up the tracks at night. Consequently, it took two days for Frank and Geoffrey Royall to get to Hantan, a journey once made in just eight hours.

In Hantan, Frank and Geoffrey boarded an old, rickety bus bound for Taming. The driver propped a notched stick between the gearshift and instrument panel to keep it in gear, often stopping to refill a leaking radiator. As they neared Taming, Frank grew more nervous about what they might see. To their delight, they were able to spot the windmill and water tower as the bus passed by the compound on its way into Taming, where they obtained clearance from the Japanese guards.

By rented rickshaw they at last approached the mission compound itself, staring in amazement at the unharmed facilities. The compound was completely intact. In contrast, the nearby army barracks and normal school lay in ruins from bombing and looting.

Suddenly, the Wieses and Chinese workers met them with beaming faces. Letters, each one severely censured, had kept Frank and Rev. Royall up-to-date on what had been happening. Now they would hear it all firsthand.

As the Japanese approached Taming, Chinese soldiers had punched holes in the mission compound wall for 75-mm cannons. Rev. Wiese responded by traveling into Taming to plead with the Chinese command to vacate the compound. Needless to say, his efforts were in vain.

On November 10, after continual air raids, Rev. Wiese persuaded Mrs. Wiese that she should take their children and go south to Chaocheng (formerly Ch'ao Ch'eng). She, along with others in the party, made the trip safely under extremely hazardous conditions.

Meanwhile, Rev. Wiese remained in Taming, and he, with several Chinese leaders, took shelter in the basement of the Wiese home, which was reinforced with sandbags around the windows. All the other residents at the mission compound fled into the countryside.

Taming fell to the Japanese invaders on November 12. A tank punched through the compound wall, and the fighting was over. When all seemed quiet, Rev. Wiese emerged from his basement shelter to ask permission from a ranking Japanese officer to bury the dead soldiers.

Japanese troops occupied Taming, but not the lawless countryside. Looters stripped everything from the normal school and army barracks. But, on entering the mission compound, they were confronted by a lone and unarmed missionary. To his surprise, they turned, fled, and did not return. Rev. Wiese's courage saved the compound and all its buildings.

After hearing Rev. Wiese's story, the missionaries could only wonder and rejoice in God's protection. Frank, along with Revs. Wiese and Royall, then went immediately to Chaocheng, where a bomb had destroyed the church. Chinese Christians received them joyfully, telling stories of God's protection from war and robbers while the missionaries encouraged the Christians and inspected the damaged church. Rev. Wiese assigned men to begin repairs.

With the summer's heat and the unsettled conditions around Taming, the Sutherland family and the other missionaries all went to Peitaiho. Located on the coast, the city is not far from where China's Great Wall comes down to the sea. Frank stayed behind in Taming.

Then, while still in Peitaiho, word came that Frank had amoebic dysentery. He was given two courses of emetine, a strong drug with heart toxicity. One day, while Mrs. Pattee was on duty, Frank lost consciousness and became pulseless. She quickly administered a stimulant that revived him, but his strength came back very slowly.

Ann and the children returned to Taming late in August, just as Frank came home from the hospital in a severely weakened state. Other missionaries helped open the Bible school, and Rev. Osborn served as the temporary director. The school accommodated only 108 students, although far more applied. In an effort to respond to the growing interest, missionaries planned a new girls' dormitory and classroom building.

During this time, the war raged on. And while the Japanese occupied Taming and other key cities on the mission field, the countryside remained under the control of the central government's 29th Route Army. These soldiers engaged in guerrilla warfare, burning and blowing up bridges and continuously probing for weaknesses they might exploit. At night, the missionaries frequently heard rifle fire. One night Frank heard a bullet hit the side of the Sutherland house. They found it the next morning half buried in a brick.

Even in the midst of such difficult days, the Sutherlands experienced the blessings and peace of God in unexpected but welcomed ways. That Christmas, students at Northwest Nazarene College surprised the Sutherlands with many presents. The gifts required a special cart to bring them home from the post office in Taming. The family spent several hours opening the presents amid squeals of delight and amazement at the generosity of the students. As always, Frank and Ann thanked God for His provisions.

Once again, the missionaries sensed another window of opportunity. The Pattees went to Chengan, and the Royalls went to Chaocheng. The hospital treated more and more patients, and the Bible school, according to Ann, was "humming." The demand for Bibles and Christian literature increased, and Ann kept ordering more from the publishers to keep a supply on hand.

Remembering Hosea's lament, "My people are destroyed from lack of knowledge" (4:6), Bible school students were sent out during the summer of 1939 across the Nazarene district. They held doctrinal classes among both older Christians and new inquirers. Some were from a background of total ignorance of the gospel, but all were eager to learn. The students returned from these mission trips with enthusiastic reports of their experiences, and everyone praised God for His protection.

Frank rejoiced over these dedicated and industrious young students, remarking in a letter, "Our hearts are encouraged for the future."

Ann worked with evangelistic bands formed among the Bible students and accompanied teams of young women as they cycled out to the villages on Sunday afternoons. Shortly after the Chinese New Year, 20 young women formed four or five bands to go out alone, their cycles bearing pennants with Bible verses. They went to churches to spend a week or so in evangelism, with a great deal of prayer preceding their efforts. The women returned from these trips, as Ann wrote, "bubbling over with experiences to tell. At Nazarene Young People's Society they all reported at a joyful service that lasted two hours and a half!"

Later that year, Dr. and Mrs. Henry Wesche and their daughter Mary returned to work at the hospital, bringing Arthur and Blanche Moses along as well. Arthur became the hospital business manager, and Blanche took over nurses' training.

As the war in Europe escalated in 1940, the war in China seemed to drag on. On the diplomatic front, the United States government resisted the Japanese effort to dominate the Far East. The consulates of Britain and the United States continued to warn citizens living in China that they could not guarantee their safety.

Frank was determined to continue with the Bible school as long as possible because of the many fine students who would be future leaders of the Chinese church. Ann continued to teach the older women to read, supervise the Chinese children in

Sunday School, and assist the female Bible students with their evangelistic bands. Every ministry seemed to be bearing fruit.

GRADUATING CLASS OF 1939

GRADUATING CLASS OF 1940

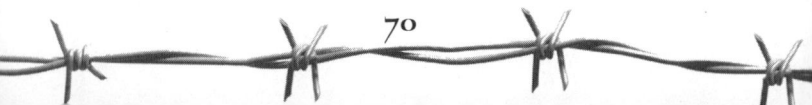

In the meantime, missionaries of other denominations and other foreigners were leaving China, as it seemed the United States might be drawn into the war. There were not enough ships to take everyone desiring to leave, so the U.S. Navy sent a troop transport to help get Americans out of the country. At about that time, Japanese officers came out of Taming to visit the mission and told Frank, "Our countries will be at war soon."

MISSIONARIES SERVING IN CHINA IN 1940. (FIRST ROW, LEFT TO RIGHT) PAULINE WIESE (HOLDING HER SISTER LAURA MAE), MARY WESCHE, MARGARET SUTHERLAND, ELLEN SUTHERLAND, RUTH MOSES, PHYLLIS PATTEE, FRANCIS SUTHERLAND, PAUL SUTHERLAND, BOBBIE PATTEE, CLARENCE WIESE. (SECOND ROW) MISS EVELYN EDDY, MISS MARY PANNELL, MRS. MABEL WESCHE, MRS. ANN SUTHERLAND, MRS. BLANCHE MOSES (HOLDING HER DAUGHTER CAROL), MRS. LILLIAN PATTEE, DR. HESTER HAYNE, PAUL ROYALL, MRS. ANN ROYALL (HOLDING HER DAUGHTER EVANGELINE), MRS. EMMA OSBORN. (THIRD ROW) DR. HENRY WESCHE, REV. HARRY WIESE, MRS. KATHERINE WIESE (HOLDING HER SON JAMES), REV. FRANK SUTHERLAND, MR. ARTHUR MOSES, REV. JOHN PATTEE, MISS RHODA SCHURMAN, REV. GEOFFREY ROYALL, REV. LEON OSBORN.

Chapter 13
LEAVING CHINA

By *early 1941*, Hitler's armies occupied much of Europe. His submarines, operating in wolf packs, thwarted British shipping efforts in the North Atlantic. Meanwhile, the American and British Consulates continually pressured their citizens to get out of China.

The missionaries, through long hours of prayer, agonized over what they should do. They wanted to continue the work, which seemed to be going so well. After only a few years, the Bible school already had graduates pastoring churches. God was powerfully at work through Nazarene missionaries, planting His gospel in the fertile land north of the Yellow River in North China.

Several questions raced through their minds. How would their leaving affect the Chinese Christians, so new in their faith? Would they feel abandoned?

Finally, the China Missionary Council, with Department of Foreign Missions' approval, decided the Royalls, the Pattees, Mary Pannell, Evelyn Eddy, and the Sutherlands, whose terms were actually completed, should return home. The board left it up to the rest as to what they should do. John Pattee decided to stay, although his family returned home. Leon and Emma Osborn, Arthur Moses, and Mary Scott, whose terms were not up, also decided to stay. Mrs. Mabel Wesche and Blanche Moses decided to leave, and Dr. Henry Wesche stayed until a Chinese physician, Dr. Liu, joined the staff that summer.

For Frank and Ann the decision was not easy. Frank felt especially burdened for the Bible school. He had reopened it just five years earlier and desperately wanted to stay. However, he was concerned for the safety of Ann and the five children. Ann, too, could have stayed. She had proven her courage during the first term, when she spent lonely nights as the only foreigner in Chengan with robbers and rogue soldiers roaming the countryside.

Frank's background in history and his keen knowledge of world affairs convinced him that Japan would soon be at war with both Britain and the United States. To stay would mean becoming prisoners of war. Also, they hadn't seen John and David for five years. Should they be imprisoned, how many more years would it be? With a sense of peace from God, Frank and Ann decided to leave.

To prepare for departure, the trunks were brought down from the third floor attic. They decided to leave their furniture for future missionaries after the war. Little did they know, those future missionaries would not be allowed to come.

Spring only hinted at arriving on the morning of March 1, 1941, leaving the air dry, dusty, and chilly under a brightly shining sun. Many Christians, the hospital staff, and Chinese servants lined the circular drive that connected the homes of the missionaries in the mission compound. The missionaries and their children climbed into the Royalls' light blue

1936 Chevrolet panel truck and the Osborns' royal blue 1938 Deluxe Chevrolet sedan. As they slowly circled the compound, the Chinese sang their version of "God Be with You [Till We Meet Again]."

After circling the loop, the group left the inner gate and drove toward the outer gate. Here, Bible school students lined the road, girls on one side and boys on the other. At the end of each line a student held aloft a standard bearing a triangular silk banner that floated above the cars as they passed underneath. The banners proclaimed a farewell message in Chinese calligraphy characters. They gave these as mementos to the departing missionaries. It would be the last time on earth Frank and Ann would see the students who bid them farewell that chilly spring morning.

The cars moved out of the compound gate and onto the auto road. They traveled to Hantan, where they would board the train for Peking. Attached to each car was a large American flag in case Chinese soldiers along the route should mistake them for Japanese.

Getting a ship to the United States was not easy, as many Americans were returning home. No tourist class vacancies were available, but they were finally able to book third-class tickets on the SS *President Cleveland* of the American President Line. Third-class cabins had bunks stacked four high, navy fashion, with eight people to a cabin and were the traditional choice of third-world nationals. The steamship line allowed missionaries traveling third class to eat in the tourist class dining rooms. This made the 21 days at sea from Shanghai to San Francisco more pleasant.

Two days out of Shanghai, the *Cleveland* passed a fleet of Japanese warships on maneuvers. A destroyer quickly laid a smoke screen, hiding the others. Frank's concern for their position was heightened as war threatened to break out. Fortunately, each day took them farther from troubled China and menacing warships. Now, the tropical paradise of Hawaii and, beyond that, the United States lay ahead.

As they approached Honolulu, a coast guard cutter met and trailed the *Cleveland* into harbor to ensure that narcotics were not dropped overboard to be picked up by small boats from the shore. They steamed past the entrance to Pearl Harbor Naval Base, past "battleship row," and into Honolulu harbor, docking near the Aloha Tower. They would depart for San Francisco the next day.

Chapter 14
HOME AGAIN

As the ship from Hawaii neared the Golden Gate Bridge, passengers lined the deck railings. They peered through the fog to catch sight of the newly built bridge whose construction the Sutherland children had seen in the pages of *National Geographic.* Finally, they caught a glimpse of the reddish brown structure seemingly suspended in air above the fog. They passed under it, sailed around the prison island of Alcatraz, and on toward the white buildings and houses of San Francisco. Finally, nudged by two tugs, they docked at Pier 42 along the Embarcadero.

The Sutherlands proved too many for one home and were sent to stay with two Nazarene families in Berkeley before going on to Nampa. In these homes, small things brought great pleasure. Cornflakes with cow's milk topped by cream and poured from glass bottles tasted so good in comparison with the cooked cereals and goat's milk of China.

On the negative side, Frank was astonished at the extent to which Americans failed to realize the dangers of what was going on in the world. Frank and Ann also sensed that the United States underestimated Japan's ability to wage war. They had seen the Japanese soldiers who occupied China and knew that any war with Japan would not be easily won.

✳ ✳ ✳

Waiting in Nampa, John and David heard the deep-throated whistle of the passenger train, and the huge black steam engine appeared in the distance. As the engineer pulled back the throttle, wisps of steam jetted out from the massive pistons. The train braked slowly to a stop, as John and David searched the faces stepping off the train. Their gaze soon locked onto parents and younger brothers and sisters, all five years older than John and David remembered. The Sutherlands were reunited.

That fall, for the third time, Frank became Prof. F. C. Sutherland. As a professor of history at Northwest Nazarene College (NNC), Frank's favorite period was the Reformation. Former students (now Revs.) John Bullock and Floyd Perkins remember vividly his emotional description of this great turning point in history.

The war Frank feared soon started. After dinner, on December 7, 1941, NBC's H. V. Kaltenborn broke into programming over radio station KIDO in Boise, Idaho, announcing in his staccato voice, "Ladies and gentlemen . . . I have an important announcement . . . from the White House. . . . The Japanese have attacked . . . Pearl Harbor!"

A radio brought into NNC's chapel service on Monday carried President Roosevelt's "Day of Infamy" speech, and World War II dominated the lives of everyone for the next four years.

Meanwhile, back in China, a Japanese officer told the missionaries still remaining in Taming about the war. The Osborns, John Pattee, Arthur Moses,

and Miss Mary Scott were taken into custody as enemy aliens. The Osborns, Rev. Pattee, and Mr. Moses were allowed to go home a few months later.

Inexplicably, the captors sent Miss Mary Scott, who came to China in 1940, to a civilian internment camp in Shangtung Province. Here, internally chosen camp leaders assigned this talented and energetic young lady to latrine duty until she was liberated by American parachutists on August 17, 1945. Miss Scott went on to become general executive secretary of the Nazarene World Mission Society.

Before the Sutherlands left China, the Eighth Route Army of Mao Tse-tung, under the joint defense agreement with the Nationalist government of Chiang Kai-shek, moved into the Nazarene mission field. Their green uniforms replaced the familiar gray ones of the Nationalist army. The Sutherland children saw this change in the villages outside Taming, then occupied by the Japanese. Following the war, the Eighth Route Army turned from fighting the Japanese to fighting the Nationalists for control of all China.

The Communist government did not allow foreign missionaries into their areas of control. Consequently, the Department of Foreign Missions was left without a field in China. Nevertheless, mission headquarters explored possibilities for a new field in South China, which was beyond Communist control. After some initial contact, Nazarene missionaries arrived in Kian, Kiangsi Province, a thousand miles south of Taming.

Hoping to start a Bible school in South China, the board commissioned Frank and Ann to return to

China in 1948. They would join the Pattees, Miss Ruth Brickman, the Fitzes, Miss Mary Scott, and the Michael Varros, already in Kian. But before they could set sail, Miss Scott wrote a letter describing the uncertainties facing the work in China. Communists and Nationalists were fighting at Hsu Chow. Hankow or Nanking would likely be next.

In spite of the ongoing war, God continued to bless the work. Five hundred students signed slips of intent to become Christians at a Youth for Christ meeting, and another 100 came to the Nazarene mission in Kian to pick up copies of the Gospel of John. Chinese pastors and Bible school students from the north found their way to Kiangsi to join the work in South China.

One minister wrote to Frank seven years after he and the other students bid the Sutherlands farewell in Taming. Written in Chinese calligraphy, his letter told a heroic story of teaching in a school and winning students for Jesus until the coming of the Communists. The Communists forced him into military service, but he managed to escape. Hiding in a believer's home in the mountains, he eventually made his way to Kiangsi to join Revs. Wiese and Pattee. He prayed, simply, that he might be a "fit vessel."

The China Mission Council, with General Superintendent Orval Nease's approval, recommended that the Sutherlands delay their departure until a more propitious time. That time never came. The Communists soon took control of all of China, forcing closure of the work in South China and the evacuation of our missionaries.

Frank remained at NNC, retiring from active

teaching in 1960 to become the college archivist. In 1957 NNC granted Frank an honorary degree, Doctor of Laws; and in 1960, the Church of the Nazarene awarded him a Citation of Merit at the General Assembly. Editors of the *Oasis*, NNC's annual, dedicated three issues to Prof. F. C. Sutherland: 1930, 1944, and 1950. During NNC's 75th Anniversary Celebration, former students selected Frank as "Professor of the 1920s Decade."

In 1970 cancer required Frank to undergo surgery for intestinal obstruction. Postoperatively, the obstruction remained. Frank maintained his cheerfulness despite living in much pain and discomfort until his death later that year. An attending nurse at Nampa's Mercy Medical Center commented, "I've just watched a Christian die."

Ann lived alone after Frank's death. Throughout this period, she remained an active member of College Church in Nampa, serving on the Communion Committee and in the missionary society. She belonged to Faculty Femmes, wives of NNC faculty members, and she also served in the Women's Christian Temperance Union. The Sage Brush Club, a social group that visited historical and scenic sites in the Boise Valley, allowed her to explore the outdoors as she had enjoyed doing years earlier on the slopes of Mount Newton.

Ann also visited her sister Ellen in New Jersey annually. Then, as her health began to fail, she reluctantly moved out of the home and into Sunnyridge Manor, a retirement center just south of Nampa. After a short time, she was no longer able to care for herself and was moved into the nursing unit. For a few years, she was totally dependent on the skilled and compassionate nursing staff headed by Mrs. Sharon Wise Skillings. The daughter of African missionaries John and Marjorie Wise, Sharon made these last years comfortable for Ann until 1987, when she joined Frank in heaven.

FRANK AND ANN SUTHERLAND AFTER RETIREMENT

Frank and Ann are now members of the Church Triumphant. We can only wonder about their joys of being reunited with each other and with old friends and fellow workers. There is no doubt that Frank and Ann are celebrating God's grace with Chinese pastors who were once Bible school students. Former students and faculty colleagues from NNC are likely talking about revivals, out-of-debt campaigns, and the influence of NNC alumni around the world.

The seven Sutherland children are all active in their respective churches. They remember their parents as two people deeply in love with each other and with their children. Frank and Ann were also totally dedicated to the work of the Lord and to the part of God's kingdom called the Church of the Nazarene. By their example, they instilled a love for Jesus and His kingdom into the hearts of everyone they touched.

EPILOGUE

by A Friend of China

What a story! As a Christian and member of the Church of the Nazarene who lives and ministers in the Greater China area, I rejoice each time I read an account of God's faithfulness to those He calls to serve in Chinese ministries. I read this account of God's grace at work in the lives of Frank and Ann Sutherland nonstop from beginning to end. Thankfully, there is more to the story. It is time for an update.

China's people, 23 percent of the world's population, have experienced an enormous amount of change since our missionaries left China. Mainland China's Christians have lived through events impossible to understand from an outsider's perspective. Even for someone who has lived and worked in China, these events are difficult to describe. China has struggled through cycles of change.

Also, since the departure of missionaries such as Frank and Ann Sutherland, mission policy and missionary practices have changed. In recent decades, most missionaries have chosen to live with the people rather than on mission compounds. Today, most missionary-sending agencies have policies that direct missionaries to cooperate with directives from national embassies in host nations. But in spite of their significance, these changes are not of primary importance to the update.

The question burning in the minds of so many Christians outside of mainland China is, "What has happened to the church, to our Christian brothers and sisters, since the days of the Japanese invasion and China's own civil war?" Nazarenes have prayed for China's church in general and especially for the church planted in the Taming area—an area just south of Beijing. Unfortunately, our missionaries were not able to return to the Taming field. They never had an opportunity to continue to minister with their Chinese friends and colleagues in the designated Nazarene field.

When our missionaries left China for the last time, there were 54 organized churches, dozens of church plants, 5,500 members and probationary members, and 163 Bible college students left under the superintendency of God's Holy Spirit. For everyone who has longed to know what happened to this formidable ministry, the following is a brief update. Rejoice! As you read, listen with the ears of your heart. You will hear mainland China's Christians, including those who share our heritage, cry out, "Jesus keeps His promises!"

The Church of Mainland China Since 1941

In 1949, under the leadership of Chairman Mao, the Chinese Communist Party placed its ironclad grip over all of mainland China. The new government forced all Christian missionaries to leave mainland China by 1951. It is estimated that at the time, the Christian population of mainland China was just over 5 million. These brave believers in Christ continued to serve our Lord behind the invisible bamboo curtain.

In 1951 the Chinese Communist Party established a new agency, the Three-Self Patriotic Movement, to govern the Christian movement across the great land of China. Churches willing to register with the government were required to live within government restrictions. As for the rest, the government began to systematically close all churches not willing to register.

In the Bible (e.g., Daniel and the Acts of the Apostles), God calls His people to corporate worship, to evangelize those who do not know our Lord, to disciple new believers, and to expand the kingdom of God. In obedience, China's underground house church movement began to expand across China as the Church Militant.

From 1966 through 1976, under the leadership of Chairman Mao, his wife Jiang Ching, and the other members of the so-called Gang of Four, China suffered a great tragedy—the Cultural Revolution. For 10 years Mao and Jiang whipped the Red Guard, the teenagers of China, into a frenzy. Mao and Jiang, the architects of the Cultural Revolution, repeatedly sent the Red Guard out to ravage their own homeland. They destroyed works of art as well as the artists themselves. They wasted pieces of music, musical instruments, and musicians; ravaged educational facilities and tortured their own teachers; and in many instances persecuted their own parents, siblings, and extended family members. The Red Guard, supported by Chairman Mao, the Gang of Four, and the military, also looted and locked up religious facilities while persecuting many Christians. The blood of Christian martyrs fell on the seed of the gospel of Jesus Christ.

By the end of the Cultural Revolution in 1976, the Red Guard had successfully closed every church, even those that had agreed to register with the government during the period following 1951. On the surface, there was not a single place in all of mainland China where our Christian brothers and sisters were allowed to openly worship the Lord.

Two thousand years before Chairman Mao and the Gang of Four, 2,000 years before the Chinese Communist Party erected the bamboo curtain around the world's most populous nation, 2,000 years before the great chaos of the Cultural Revolution swept across China like a dark, destructive storm, 2,000 years before the blood of China's Christians flowed, Jesus Christ looked His disciples squarely in the eyes and made a promise, saying, "I will build my church; and the gates of hell shall not prevail against it" (Matt. 16:18, KJV).

The underground house church, China's Church Militant, marched on, and her ranks increased at record pace. What started as a quiet trickle had now become a mighty, rushing, underground river—the exciting, exploding, and expanding underground house church movement of mainland China!

By 1977 Chairman Mao had died. The Gang of Four resided in four prison cells in Beijing. Local officials began to allow limited numbers of registered churches to once again welcome Christians to corporate worship. Today, all across China, Christians in the registered state churches refer to this event as the "resurrection of the church." I celebrate with them every time I hear this phrase.

In spite of the turning tide, the state church remains limited. Today, over 20 years since the end of the Cultural Revolution, there are less than 10 registered churches in Beijing (the booming national capital is home to over 11 million people). And in these churches, the government designates who serves as pastor, where the church can meet, and what times are appropriate for worship. The government must also approve the content of each worship service, and evangelizing people who have not reached their 18th birthday is strictly illegal.

However, some local officials choose to allow registered churches greater freedom. When and where this happens, many of the registered churches have become thriving, growing, and expanding congregations. These churches recognize their role, as the Body of Christ, to serve as salt and light in a very needy world. Praise the Lord!

In 1992 Beijing's State Bureau of Statistics sent out a team of surveyors across China to answer the following question: "How many Christians are there in China?" The team returned to Beijing with an amazing report. In response to the government's regulations and the Cultural Revolution, the 1949 Christian population of just over 5 million (1.8 million Protestants; 3.3 million Catholics) had grown to 75 million (63 million Protestants; 12 million Catholics) in 1992 (*Operation World*, 164). A. Brent Cobb, Asia-Pacific regional director, indicates that there are probably 90 to 100 million Christians today.

Of course, accepting these amazing facts is difficult for an atheistic government. The official government statement suggests there are about 8 million Christians in China's registered churches. But only about 13 percent of China's Christians affiliate with the registered churches.

A Report from Taming

In early December 1996, winter blasted the rich farmlands of eastern China. Two Chinese women, one 18 years of age, the other 20, made their way through the darkness.

On an overcast night the farmlands of China are very dark—a 40-watt bulb now and then offers little relief. The young women leaned into the wind. The temperature was 15 degrees Fahrenheit, and snow was blowing. They wore heavy boots and several layers of clothing, topped off with heavy parkas, the hoods drawn up around coal-black eyes. As they neared each dim light, they hoped it designated their final destination. They hoped they had correctly followed the handwritten directions sent weeks earlier.

With each step, the snow and ice crunched under their feet. Finally, about midnight, as they approached yet another dim light, they made out the silhouette of a man standing out in the blizzard near the entrance to a farmhouse. One whispered through dry lips, "I hope he is the watchman." They slowed their pace, hoping he would notice them. The watchman saw them coming and motioned for them to approach. They said the appointed words. The watchman, hearing those words, knew they belonged inside. He waved for them to enter the farmhouse.

Between 12 midnight and 2 A.M., 26 more house church pastors made their way through the darkness and the blizzard to the farmhouse. The watchman allowed them to enter one by one.

In eastern China, pastors meet every three months to receive instruction from invited teachers, Chinese pastors from other areas who have been privileged to receive more thorough biblical training. The guest teachers help them deal with the false teachings that plague the house church movement—false teachings that exist because the church has expanded for over 40 years with little or no Scripture in hand.

These pastors, and the many pastors and Christians they represent, are of particular interest to Nazarenes. They represent the church that Nazarene missionaries planted in the Taming area.

From 2 A.M. until 2:30 A.M., 28 house church pastors waited for their invited guest. They had invited me to participate in that evening's training session. They had two purposes in mind, as follows: They wanted to study a specific holiness theme, and they wanted to report to me what God Almighty had done at the grassroots level of the church since 1941. What a humbling privilege and responsibility.

What a trip! After 14 hours of travel, I followed three house church leaders down a dark, frozen road. The only sounds were our heavy breathing and the crunch of snow and ice under our boots. At 2:30 A.M. we entered the farmhouse where 28 house church pastors were waiting in prayer. What a warm welcome—firm handshakes, broad smiles, and words of encouragement. As we prepared for a very cold night of sleep, the walls of that farmhouse seemed to drip with anticipation and the presence of the One who had called us together.

The next morning, following a delicious breakfast sacrificially prepared for all of the pastors by local Christians, we began 14 hours of training and reporting. We worked our way through the apostle Paul's letter to the Christians in Rome, seeking answers for many questions regarding holiness.

The highlight was hearing their report of what God Almighty had done in that area since our missionaries left in 1941. Their testimonies included emotional witness to the Spirit's inner strength, detailed accounts of God's call to pastoral ministry, humbling witness to His presence during months of imprisonment, vivid replays of evangelistic church planting events, and accounts of miracles that had glorified God and drawn nonbelievers to our Lord.

I began to ask questions about numbers of churches and Christians. These pastors, whose zeal for evangelism and church planting makes the air thick with expectant hope, humbly hesitated to speak of numbers. I told them that our church at home would be greatly encouraged by such a report. I offer the following summary of their report. The statistics are only estimates—conservative estimates.

The Sutherlands and other Nazarene missionaries planted a church that understood, among other things, the church exists to expand the kingdom of God through evangelism and church planting. The number of registered state churches and underground house churches in that tiny corner of mainland China probably exceeds 1,000! One man supervises 60 churches within a small county. Another man is the leader of over 200 churches in another county—each church pastored by a local believer. These are but two examples of the explosive growth the house church has experienced in our former field and other areas of eastern China.

My next question concerned the number of Christians in the area where Nazarene missionaries sowed the seed of the gospel of Christ. Their reports confirmed the information received in the 1980s, when Dr. George Rench and Dr. John Holstead, men who served in Chinese ministries in Taiwan, Hong Kong, and mainland China, met with local officials. Then, in 1989, Rev. John Pattee and a professor from Asia-Pacific Nazarene Theological Seminary enjoyed a few days in Taming. One government official told Rev. Pattee, who maintained fluency in Mandarin up through the age of 90, that there may be 70,000 Christians in the Taming area with roots in the Church of the Nazarene.

This is one example of how the Spirit of God has made the gospel seed planted across China amazingly fruitful. Remember the infant church that our missionaries were forced to leave in 1941? Fifty-four organized churches have expanded to exceed 1,000! Five thousand five hundred Christians now exceed 70,000!

Take time right now to worship our Lord. In your own way praise the One who promises, "I will build my church; and the gates of hell shall not [stand] against it" (Matt. 16:18, KJV).

* * *

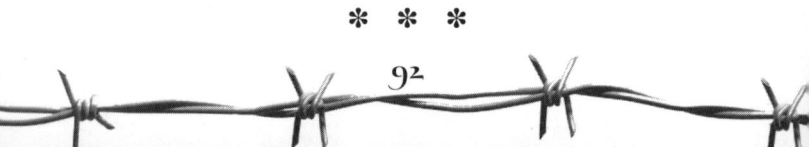

Fifty hours passed much too quickly. A closing prayer turned into a lengthy time of spontaneous worship and praise. Then it was time to depart. For the first time in 50 hours I exited the door I had entered during the blizzard. The blizzard had blown over.

One of the men transported me on the back of a bicycle. We made our way through the near total darkness and absolute silence of the sleeping farm community. The only constant sound was the crunch of snow under the bicycle's tires. After some minutes of silence, the man whispered over his shoulder, "Brother, thank the church who sent the missionaries. Tell them what God has done in this place."

I wanted to cry out in full voice, but I silently cried out in my spirit, "Jesus! Thank You for these brave, obedient Christians. May the Spirit who empowers them empower me! May the Spirit who leads them lead me! May the Spirit who pushes them out in Kingdom-expanding activities keep pushing me out!"

With the ears of my heart, I could hear Jesus calling down through the halls of history, "I told you. I made a promise. I will build My Church."

Can you hear them? Can you hear the Christians of mainland China? Can you hear our brothers and sisters in the Taming area? They cry out words to encourage and challenge all of us, saying, "Jesus keeps His promises!"

PRONUNCIATION GUIDE

The following information is provided to assist in pronouncing Chinese and other unfamiliar words in the book. The suggested pronunciations, though not precise, are close approximations of the way the terms are pronounced in English.

Beijing	BAY-JING
Chaocheng	CHOW-CHUNG
Chengan	CHUNG-AN
Chiang Kai-shek	JUNG KIE-SHEHK
Fanshien	FAN-SEE-EHN
Fen Yu Hsiang	FUNG YOO SEE-AHNG
Feng	FUNG
Hai Ho	HIE HOH
Hankow	HAN-KOW
Hantan	HAHN-DAHN
Honan	HOH-NAN
Hopei	HUH-BAY
Hsu Chow	SHOO-CHOW
Jiang Ching	JING CHING
Jong Tso Lin	JAHNG SOH LIHN
Kian	JEE-UNG
Kiangsi	JEE-UNG-SHEE
Kiehn	KEEN
koaliang	GAHL-ee-ahng
Kwancheng	KWAHN-CHUNG
Liu	LOO
Manchu	MAN-CHOO
Mao Tse-tung	MOW suh-DUNG
Mei-ling	MAY-LING

Nanking	NAN-KING
Nanlo	NAN-LOW
Peitaiho	BAY-duh-HUH
Peking	PEE-KING
Shanghai	SHUNG-HIE
Shantung	SHAN-DOONG
Soong	SOONG
Sun Yat-sen	SUN YAHT-SEHN
Ta Ku	TAH GOO
Taming	DAH-MING
Tientsin	TYEHN-SIN
Tsinan	ZEE-NAN
Tsingtao	CHING-DOW
Wei	WAY
Wesche	WES-shee
Wiese	WEE-see
Yangtze	YUNG-SEE
Yu	YOO

Sources: Robert Sutherland and *Merriam-Webster's Collegiate®
Dictionary, 10th edition.*

Marie Whetstone 5-30-99
S B Whetstone 6-1-99
M Houghlin 7-10-99
Tracy Jackson 8·11·99